BERTIE THE BUS

STORY BY INGRID PITT
ILLUSTRATED BY ULLA REQUE
BERTIE CREATED BY TONY VLASSOPULO
SONG BY: BARRY MASON

PRINTED BY THE SPASTICS SOCIETY, MEADWAY WORKS, BIRMINGHAM.

1SBN O 9502907 3 4

BERTIE THE BUS

Jonathan watched Grandpa snoring in the shade of the big oak tree.

It wasn't very exciting and what Jonathan wanted more than anything was an adventure.

He stood up and looked across the field. At the other end was a little clump of trees. As Jonathan looked he fancied he saw something flash in the sunlight. Curious to see what it was Jonathan ran quickly across the field.

As he came closer he could see something in the shadows. He drew nearer and then stopped in surprise.

"It's a bus!" he said aloud. Jonathan went to the door and looked in.

A shrill scream rang out and a terrible white flapping shape flew straight into his face.

Jonathan staggered back and fell over. As the white fury ran off through the trees Jonathan laughed. It had only been a hen roosting in the comfortable bus.

The inside of the bus was very dirty and covered with dust and feathers. A couple of field mice stuck their heads out of a tear in one of the seats. On the back seat was a birds nest with three baby birds in it.

Jonathan went back to the front of the bus and climbed into the drivers seat. The steering wheel was so big that he could hardly reach across it with his arms and his feet were nowhere near the pedals.

He remembered all the stories Grandpa told about when he drove a bus on the busy streets of the city.

Jonathan peered out through the dirty windows at the trees crowding in on all sides.

"What's a London bus doing here?" he asked himself aloud.

Jonathan was startled when the bus shuddered and a sigh came from the engine.

"You may well ask." said a deep, sad voice. Jonathan jumped up from the seat and looked around.

BERTIE
LONDON TRANSPORT

Suddenly the dark trees cutting out the sunshine frightened him. He jumped down from the bus.

"That's right, run away. Nobody ever ran away when I was young and strong." the voice said bitterly.

"Just the opposite, in fact. All day long everybody ran after me. Oh yes. Everyone wanted Bertie then." The voice definitely came from the bus.

"I'm sorry." Jonathan said, feeling a bit foolish and looking around to make sure that nobody could see him talking to a bus.

"It's just that I didn't know buses could talk." he apologised.

The bus gave a snort that sounded like the engine being started.

"That's the trouble with people. They never listen. Only to themselves and most of the time what they say isn't worth listening to so I don't know why they do."

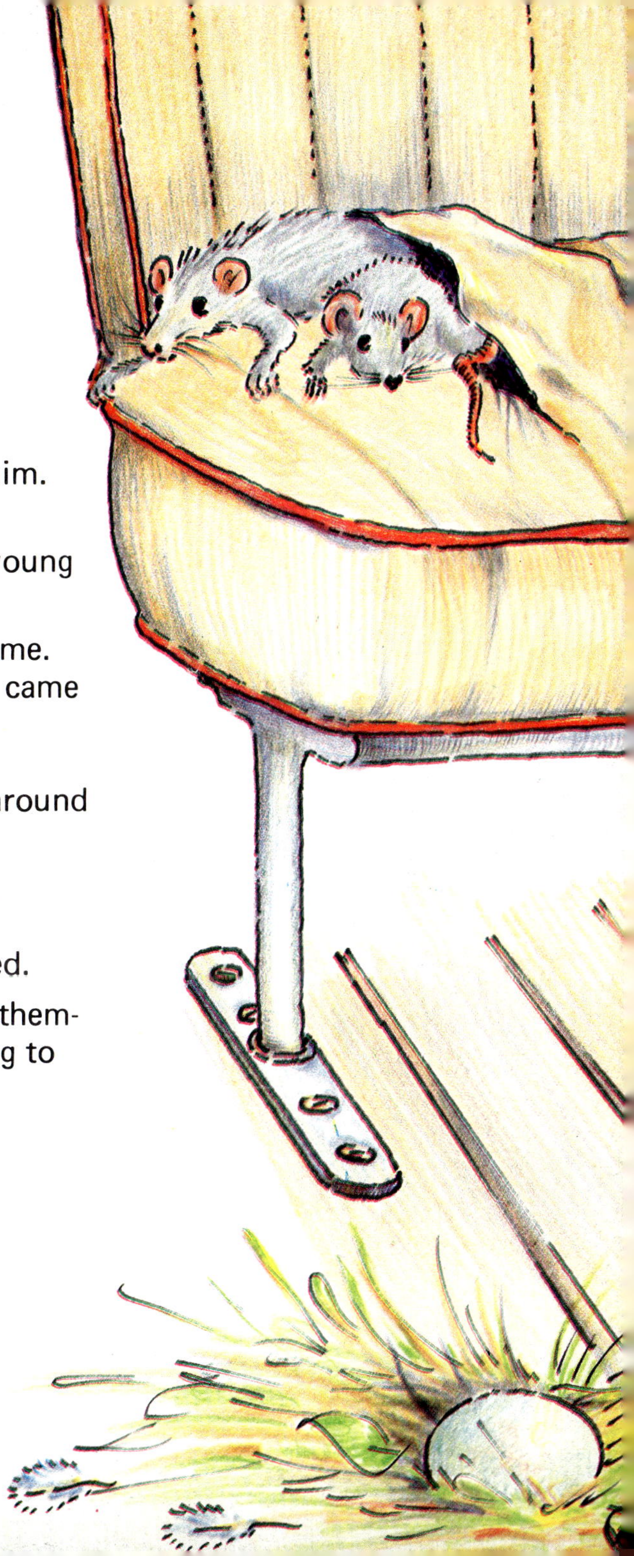

Jonathan didn't want to argue so he changed the subject.

"If you don't like it here why do you stay?" he asked.

The bus gave a shudder that made the dust fly.

"Look at me. How could I possibly let myself be seen on the road in this state?" The voice sounded as if it was going to break into tears.

"Perhaps I could help clean you up and things." Jonathan said quickly.

There was a pause and Jonathan could feel the bus looking him over.

"You are a bit small boy. What's your name?" the bus demanded.

Jonathan thought the bus could have been a bit more happy about his offer.

"Jonathan." he said defiantly. "And if you don't want my help you can stay here and look after the chickens. Good-bye." Jonathan turned and walked off.

He hadn't gone very far when the bus called after him.

"Don't go. I'm sorry."

Jonathan slowly walked back.

"What's your name?" he asked.

There was a sound like the engine trying to start again.

"Well," the voice said. "When I was working everyone called me Bertie – the Bus."

"Okay Bertie, I'll bring a bucket and some water tomorrow and we will soon have you cleaned up." he promised.

"We?" said Bertie.

"I'm sure Grandpa will want to help when I tell him about you." Jonathan said.

"I doubt it." Bertie replied. "Grown ups are the worst."

"Grandpa's different," Jonathan told Bertie. "He used to drive a bus just like you."

"Used to drive a bus, eh?" Bertie sounded interested. "Well, if you are sure he won't go telling everybody, it's alright."

Jonathan waved to Bertie as he walked off through the trees.

"See you in the morning, Bertie." he called back but the bus didn't answer.

When Jonathan told Grandpa about his adventure the old man wasn't surprised.

Next day Grandpa and Jonathan walked across the field loaded with buckets of soapy water, brushes and dusters.

Grandpa walked slowly around the bus patting it and running his hands over it as if it were a well-loved pony.

Jonathan thought Bertie liked it although he still didn't say anything.

Bertie had an effect on Grandpa too. Suddenly his eyes were brighter and his step lighter as he swung aboard and sat in the driver's seat. Jonathan was surprised to see tears in Grandpa's eyes as he got down from the bus.

BERTIE
55

LONDON
RANSPORT

"Poor old bus," he said. "Poor old bus. Something has got to be done about it. What do you call it, Jonathan?"

"Bertie". Jonathan piped up although he was listening to the whispered rumblings coming from the bus's engine.

"Well, get on with it!" Bertie growled.

Grandpa was a bit deaf and heard nothing.

"Come on then Grandpa." Jonathan said excitedly and grabbed a brush.

While Jonathan worked on the inside Grandpa cleaned up the outside. At last they were finished.

"That only leaves the engine." Grandpa said as they stood side by side looking at Bertie's glittering paintwork.

When Grandpa opened the bonnet Jonathan thought all their work had been for nothing. Birds and small animals had dragged in twigs and straw to make warm, dry homes during the winter and it looked more like a huge, untidy nest than an engine.

Grandpa didn't seem dismayed.

It took nearly two hours to clean up the engine but at last the old man stood back and nodded with satisfaction.

"There, that looks better." he said.

"Will it go?" Jonathan wanted to know.

"Go? Of course it will go." Bertie told him coldly.

Jonathan got Grandpa to sit behind the big steering wheel.

"It won't start." Grandpa warned.

"Try it, Grandpa. Try it!" Jonathan was excited now.

Grandpa looked at him and smiled.

"Alright, but don't expect a miracle." he said.

Grandpa jabbed his strong thumb down on the starter. Bertie gave a cough and a wheeze but didn't start.

Grandpa looked sadly at Jonathan.

"There you are." he said. "It's too old and passed it I'm afraid."

As Grandpa finished speaking there was another great cough from Bertie's engine and the whole bus started to rattle.

"Too old and passed it, am I?" Bertie snarled through the sound of the engine banging and whirring.

Grandpa was so surprised by the noise of the bus starting up that he just sat there. As Bertie tried to move forward the old man grabbed the steering wheel.

"Wheeeee!" he shouted, his eyes shining. "Hold tight, Jonathan, we're off!"

As they bumped across the field and into the road Jonathan could hear Bertie's deep voice singing happily in time to his engine:

"I'm back on the road again!
Rolling along in style!
Back on the open road again
Lovin' every mile.
Feelin' good,
I'm happy now.
I've found myself a friend.
I'm wondering what we have got
waitin' 'round the bend?!"

A funny feeling came over Jonathan.
He felt as if he was flying.

He shook himself and looked at Grandpa sitting so grandly behind the steering wheel. "Grandpa. Why is the bus called Bertie?" Jonathan asked.

Grandpa didn't answer.

Jonathan was about to ask again when he noticed that something was happening outside the windows. The lane they had been speeding through only a few seconds earlier had disappeared and now the windows were filled with swirling colours which looked as if they were made of candy-floss.

He made another amazing discovery. Instead of sitting in the passenger seat behind the driver he was now driving the bus. Grandpa had disappeared!

BERTIE

Jonathan looked around quickly but could not see him anywhere.

He didn't have time to search further. The mist in front of him seemed to be clearing. Jonathan gasped with surprise.

The bus WAS flying.

Suddenly the nose of the bus pointed downward. Jonathan held onto the wheel with all his might.

As they dived steeply towards the earth he could see bright flashes and puffs of smoke.

Lower down he was able to make out long lines of soldiers and horses.

BERTIE
NDON TRANSPORT

As they skimmed over the battlefield Jonathan heard Bertie's deep voice. He seemed in a bit of a huff.

"So you want to know why I'm called Bertie, do you?" he said, grating his gears. "Disrespect!"

Angrily he whirled around in a tight loop. Jonathan tried to change the subject.

"Why are those soldiers fighting?" he asked innocently. Bertie didn't answer immediately.

He was lining up to land on a narrow dirt road on a hill above the battle.

"That's better." Bertie said with a wheeze of the opening door as he came to a stop.

"Waterloo!" he suddenly boomed out with a roar from the engine that shook the bus. Surprised Jonathan looked around expecting to see the bustling railway station where he had said good-bye to his mother when he visited Grandpa.

They were on top of a grassy hill.

"Where are the trains?" he asked cautiously.

He wished he hadn't. Bertie rattled his gear level.

"Ignoramus!" he roared. "This is the Battle of Waterloo -- 1815! Down there is the famous battle between the Duke of Wellington and Napoleon! Don't you know anything?"

Jonathan thought it wiser to keep quiet and not tell Bertie that he knew that Wellington boots were named after the famous English General.

Bertie moved off down the road towards the battle.

As they rounded a corner Jonathan saw a group of soldiers in blue tunics and white trousers at the side of the road.

When they drew nearer he could see that their splendid uniforms were muddied and blood-stained. One of the soliders saw them coming and stood directly in their path and raised his hand.

The Officer stuck his bandaged head in the door and looked at Jonathan still sitting behind the big steering wheel.

"Pardon M'sieu," he said. "Will you help me to get my men to the hospital?"

Jonathan jumped down and he helped the poor wounded men scramble onto the bus. All around them shells were bursting and the air was filled with thick smoke.

Swiftly Bertie drove through the trees until he came to a grand old Chateau. Bertie slithered to a halt outside the main door and a Sister and some Nurses rushed forward to help the wounded men out of the bus.

AV 185

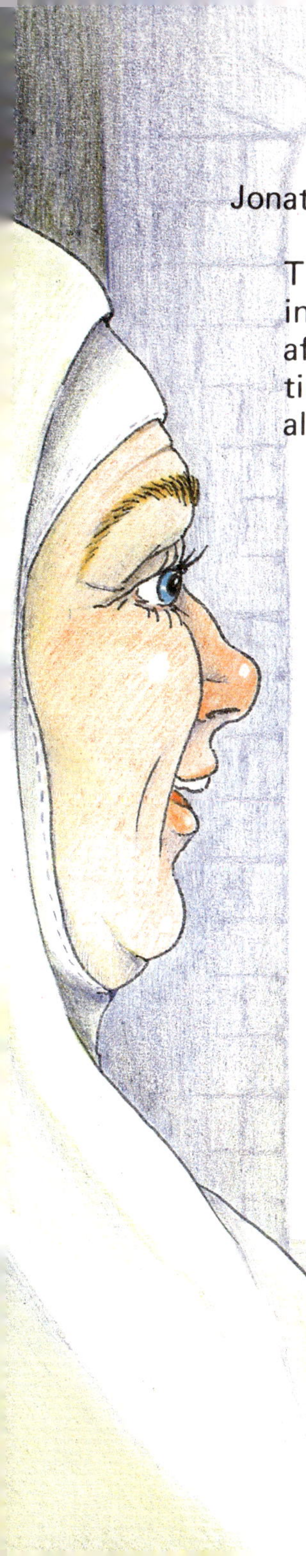

Jonathan helped too!

The rooms were crowded and Jonathan thought he had never been in such a terrible place. All day Jonathan helped the Nurses look after their patients, fetching water and winding bandages. By the time the sun began to set in the West Jonathan was so tired he was almost asleep on his feet.

Suddenly there was an air of excitement in the big ward. Jonathan stopped the Sister he had met when he first arrived. "Excuse me Sister," he said politely, "What is happening?"

The Sister gave him a quick smile and ran her hand over his untidy hair.

"The Emperor Napoleon is coming to visit the sick. Marshal Berthier will also be with him. Now run along and make yourself tidy."

Jonathan was excited. He rushed off to find Bertie to tell him the news.

Bertie had just arrived back with another group of soldiers.

"Bertie", Jonathan whispered. "Guess who's coming to visit the wounded soldiers. . . . "

Bertie gave a disdainful little rattle.

"Napoleon and Marshal Berthier, of course." he said.

Jonathan was a bit upset that Bertie already knew. He had wanted to be the one to tell him.

"How did you know?" he demanded sulkily.

Bertie released a little sniff of pressure from his airbrakes.

"Why do you think I brought you here in the first place?" he said sternly.

Before Jonathan answered there was a clatter of hooves and a group of horsemen rode up to the house where Bertie was standing. As they climbed stiffly from their horses Jonathan recognised the short, tubby little Emperor at once. Beside him was another man, tall and with a strong, hard face.

"Marshal Berthier." Bertie rattled softly to Jonathan's unspoken question

Jonathan kept down out of sight.

"Can't we leave now?" he anxiously asked Bertie. But Bertie did-not answer.

After about half an hour the French Officers came out of the Chateau and stood talking to the hospital staff in front of the bus. Jonathan hoped that they wouldn't notice him. But it was not to be.

The door slid open and the Sister stuck her head in.

"Jonathan! Are you there?" she called.

Reluctantly he stood up.

"Yes, Sister. I'm here." he muttered in a small voice.

The Sister smiled reassuringly.

"Come on out. There is someone who wants to meet you." she coaxed.

Jonathan let her pull him out of the bus door. He kept his eyes firmly on the ground determined not to look up.

It felt safer that way.

"Bertie, wake up!" he urged the sleeping bus out of the corner of his mouth.

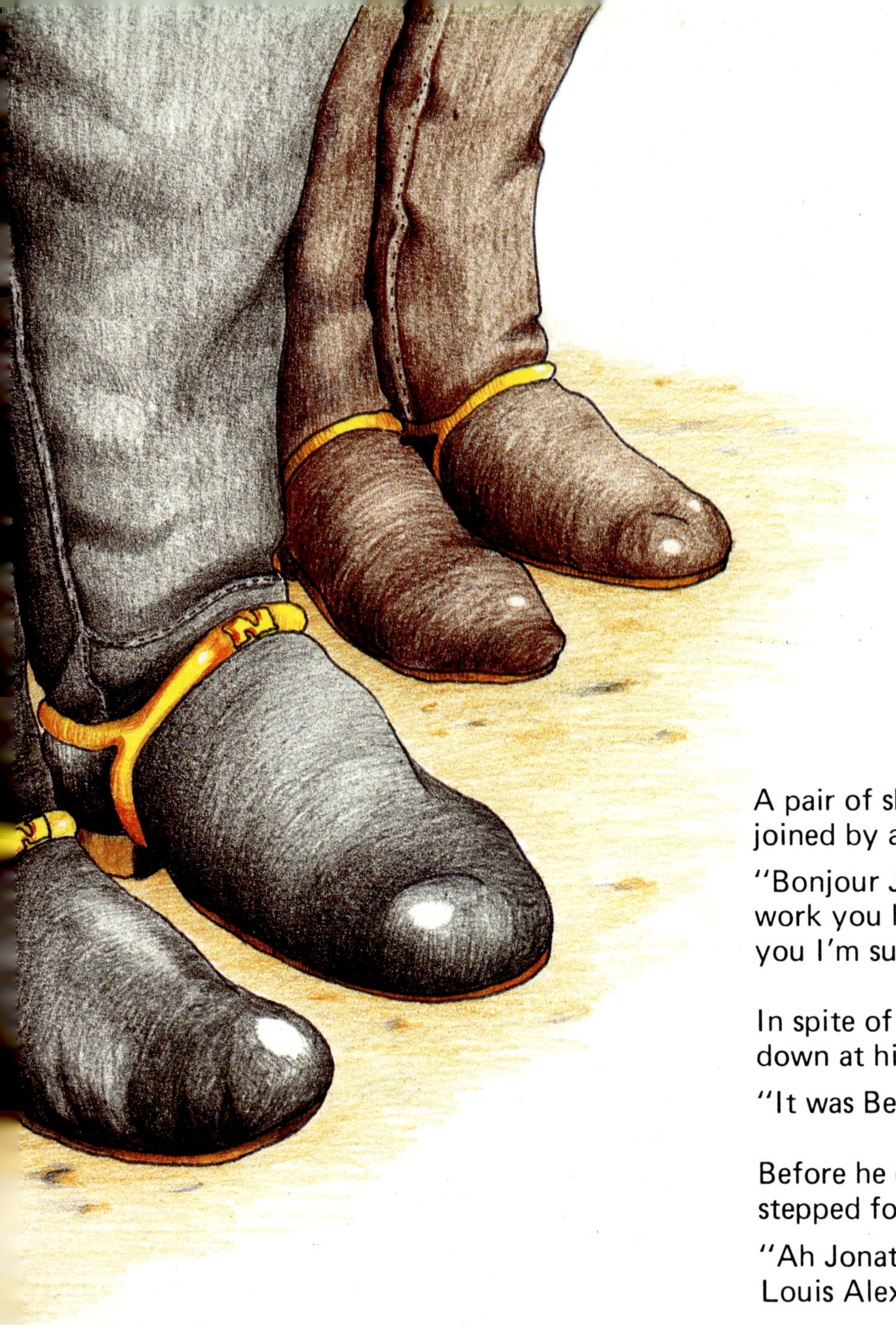

A pair of shining black boots moved into view and they were joined by a pair of brown ones. A pleasant voice spoke to him.

"Bonjour Jonathan. The Sister has told us about the wonderful work you have done with your marvellous wagon. If it wasn't for you I'm sure a lot more soldiers would have died."

In spite of himself Jonathan looked up into the dark eyes looking down at him and smiled.

"It was Bertie really." he told them. "He brought me here to see. ."

Before he could finish the tall man who had arrived with Napoleon stepped forward and the Emperor introduced him.

"Ah Jonathan. . . I would like you to meet my friend, Marshal Louis Alexandre Berthier."

The Marshal shook Jonathan's hand and stepped up to the bus and patted it.

''Bertie, eh? Such a gallant vehicle needs a grander name than that.'' he said.

Napoleon nodded and peered inside.

''You are right.''
He thought for a moment then borrowed a sword from one of his officers and stepped up to Bertie's bonnet. He tapped it lightly, first on one side and then on the other.

''For helping the sick and wounded selflessly and for showing great courage in adversity I name you after a man of equal quality — Marshal Berthier.''

The great soldier looked pleased as he walked slowly around 'Marshal Berthier' — the Bus.

As he took it Jonathan heard the sound of the bus starting up behind him.

"Time to go!" Bertie's deep voice boomed as he raced the engine.

"Thank you, Emperor!" Jonathan said and gave a deep bow from the waist, the way he had been taught at school when he was one of the Wise Men in the Christmas Play.

Emperor Napoleon and Marshal Berthier saluted smartly as he climbed aboard the bus. Jonathan waved back and hung out of the door as long as possible but Bertie was gathering speed.

"Take the wheel!" Bertie yelled as, with a hiss, the doors slammed shut and the bus seemed to leap into the air.

By the time Jonathan had struggled back to the driver's seat, the scene outside had changed to the familiar maze of crazily spinning candy-floss.

It began to fade and Jonathan could see the hedge-rows again just below him.

"Now do you know why I am called Bertie the Bus?" Bertie demanded.

Jonathan nodded.

With a chuckle Bertie changed gear and landed back in the lane.

When Jonathan recovered from the bump of the landing he was surprised to find himself sitting in the passenger seat.

"Now what are we going to do about you?" Napoleon said to Jonathan. With the sword he carefully cut one of the shiny buttons from the front of his tunic.

"Here!" He held out the button to Jonathan.

"Take this as a token of my thanks for what you have done today."

Grandpa looked round with a smile.

''Ah, you are awake now.'' he said. ''I thought you wanted to go for a ride.'' Jonathan felt disappointed. It had all been a dream!

There had been no Napoleon or Berthier and Bertie was just an ordinary old bus.

Sadly he looked out of the window. Suddenly Jonathan realised that his fingers were clasped tightly around something in the palm of his hand. Slowly he opened his fingers one by one.

He couldn't believe his eyes.

Resting there, sparkling in the afternoon sunlight, was a gold button with a big 'N' surrounded by laurel leaves carved into the surface.